P9-DDP-525

A **SporTellers**™ Book

EVE COWEN

T 31234

P

A Pacemaker® Program

Catch the Sun

Eve Cowen
AR B.L.: 3.3
Points: 1.0

UG

SporTellers™

Catch the Sun
Fear on Ice
Foul Play
High Escape
Play-Off
Race to Win
Strike Two
Stroke of Luck

Illustrator: Bob Haydock

Cover: Bob Haydock

Copyright © 1981 by Pearson Education, Inc., publishing as Globe
Fearon, an imprint of Pearson Learning Group, 299 Jefferson Road,
Parsippany, NJ 07054. All rights reserved. No part of this book may
be reproduced or transmitted in any form or by any means,
electronic, or mechanical, including photocopying, recording, or
by any information storage and retrieval system, without
permission in writing from the publisher. For information regarding
permission(s), write to Rights and Permissions Department.

ISBN 0-8224-6475-6
Printed in the United States of America

13 14 15 16 17   06 05 04 03 02

Globe
Fearon

Pearson Learning Group

1-800-321-3106
www.pearsonlearning.com

Contents

 1 Dream Come True 1

 2 Clouding Over 8

 3 Going in Circles 16

 4 Make a Bet 22

 5 Getting Set 28

 6 By the Book 32

 7 Keeping Up the Pace 38

 8 A Circle of Light 43

 9 The Marathon 48

10 The Stone Wall 54

Dream Come True **1**

Gilbert Conway was checking some papers when Deena LaSalle came into his green and white office.

"Have a seat," Conway told her. "Be with you in a second."

Deena sat down, the plans for the King Steak Restaurant in her hands. Stay calm, she told herself. She had been feeling strange all morning, as if something were about to happen. But she couldn't explain what or why.

Perhaps it was the dream she had had the night before. She had been running in the dream, but that wasn't very strange. She was a long-distance runner, and running was what she liked to do best—besides working as an architect, that is. No, the strange part of the dream was that in it she was a little girl. A little girl who ran in a cool, green forest. Had she been running toward something? Or away? She couldn't remember.

But the dream had stayed with her. Deena, like her people, the Onondaga Indians, had a great feeling for dreams. They interested her, as did the old ways and stories of her tribe. She often thought of the Onondaga reservation in upstate New York, even though she had grown up far away from it. Her home had always been in New York City. It was where she had run as a kid, not some cool forest. It was where she ran now.

Conway pushed the papers to one side of his desk, pulling Deena from her thoughts. He sat back in his chair and looked at her.

Deena ran a hand over her long, dark hair. What was the matter? she wondered. Something was going on, but what?

Conway kept looking at her. "Did you want to see me about the King Steak plans?" she finally asked. "I have them here."

"Not now," Conway said, waving them away. "I want to talk to you about something else."

Deena's heart jumped. Was it bad news? Then she squared her shoulders. She wasn't afraid of Conway. She had worked for him for seven years, and both he and she knew her work was good.

"Well, we're all set to go on the State Bank Building," he said, at last. "We've been asked to come up with some plans."

Deena's heart jumped again. Conway-Hill Architects had designed a number of sky-scrapers for cities like Houston, Chicago, and San Francisco. Not one of their skyscrapers, however, had been built in New York. So every architect in the company had hoped that Conway-Hill would be asked to design the State Bank Building that would reach toward the sky from lower Manhattan. And each one had hoped one day to point to it and say, "That's my building over there."

It was Deena's dream to say those words too.

"We really had to push hard for the OK to go ahead," Conway went on. "A lot of companies wanted the job. But the bank people know our past work and what we can do. That's why they gave us the green light."

Deena smiled. "Conway-Hill won out."

"In a way," Conway said. "But the only way we will really win is if we give them what they want."

"What they want is the most beautiful building in the world," Deena said.

Conway nodded slowly, but his next words came fast. "Think you can design it for them?" he asked.

For a few seconds, Deena could not believe her ears. Then she wanted to shout with joy. Instead, she spoke with a calm voice.

"Well, I've been giving it some thought in case we got the job," she said slowly. "Like everyone else here."

Conway pointed to the papers on his desk. "Some people have jumped the gun with ideas. I've got a desk full of their drawings already."

"I'm afraid mine are still in my head," Deena told him. "I've been too busy with the King Steak design to get anything else down on paper."

"You're finished with King Steak now. Ed James is going to take it over. So leave those plans with me. There's only one thing I want you to work on, and you know what that is."

Deena nodded. She didn't let her happy feelings show.

Now Conway turned his chair so that it faced the window behind his desk. He looked down at the busy streets of New York 27 stories below. The State Bank Building would be out there—in that forest of tall buildings.

"I want you to come up with the best plan possible," Conway began. "The building is to be a tall one—60 stories high. The spot will be between Greenwich and Beach streets."

Deena nodded again. She knew just where that was. In fact, she knew all the streets of lower New York. She had run through them often enough.

Quietly she joined Conway at the window. The sun was high, yet it didn't seem to reach the people below. Most of the streets always stayed in the shadow of the tall buildings.

Suddenly the buildings looked like staring giants. Deena surprised herself by saying, "Just what New York needs—another stone giant."

"Stone giant?" Conway looked up at her with a small smile. "That's a good thing to call them. Did you just make that up?"

"No," Deena said, laughing. "I was thinking of an old Indian legend. Something about the buildings made me remember it."

Conway turned back to the window. "Your father and brothers helped put up some of those skyscrapers. Am I right?"

"Yes, but that was a long time ago. My family is back on the reservation now."

"Perhaps they'll come back to work on your stone giant," Conway said. He seemed pleased with the idea.

Deena wondered if that would happen. Then she wondered if the opposite might happen—that she would one day live on the reservation herself. It was always in her mind.

She cleared her head and looked at Conway. He was still staring out the window. "We'll have to gobble up all those little buildings between Greenwich and Beach," he said. "This building will be the end of them."

Deena nodded her head slowly. It was a sad thought. Those little buildings let the sun in. Now a stone giant would come along and gobble them up.

"Just like the legend," she said out loud.

Conway turned and looked at her. "You'll have to tell me about that legend some day. But not right now, Deena. Now we're going to talk about a very real stone giant. Our own stone giant."

Clouding Over **2**

"What's that you just floated in on? A nice, big, soft cloud?" Flo Adams stood at the door to Deena's office and grinned at her. She was Deena's assistant—as small and round as Deena was tall and thin. "Conway liked your plans for King Steak, right? When do we get to eat there?"

"Never even talked about the plans," Deena said as she walked across the small, bright room. "In fact, it's good-bye King Steak." She sat down at her desk and began to go through her notes.

"What are you trying to tell me?" Flo asked, worried. "Are you out of a job or something?" Then she shook her head. "No, wait, that's not possible. Not when you float in here on a cloud."

Finally Deena looked up. Her face was calm and quiet. "I said good-bye to King Steak," she said to Flo. "I forgot to say hello to the State Bank skyscraper."

"What?" Flo stared at Deena, her mouth open. "You're going to design the State Bank Building? And you're sitting there calm as . . . as. . . ." Flo tried, but couldn't finish her sentence.

"I may look calm," Deena said, smiling just a little. "But inside? That's another story."

"Tell me what happened," Flo said.

"Nothing much," Deena told her. "Gilbert said, 'Would you like to try coming up with plans for the State Bank Building?' I didn't say no." Then her face clouded over for a second. "Of course, everyone else at Conway-Hill wants a crack at the building too. In fact, they've been passing on ideas to Gilbert already. You should see his desk."

Flo nodded. "But he wants you to design it, right?"

"Well, he liked the way we worked together on the skyscraper in Houston. He knows I'll be able to handle this one."

"With no help from him? Great!"

"Wait a second," Deena said. "He *is* the head of Conway-Hill. He'll still have the last say. And the first one too, for that matter."

Flo moved to the window behind Deena's desk. "There are going to be a lot of jealous architects around this place," she said, staring out at the tall buildings in front of her.

"Look, I'm not going to think about them," Deena said. "I'm only going to think about one thing—showing Gilbert Conway he was right in giving me the bank building."

"He was, and he knows it," Flo said, turning back to Deena.

Deena looked at her watch. "Two o'clock! Where did the time go? I have to get going."

"On the plans, you mean."

"No," Deena said, standing up. She pulled out a change of clothes from her drawer. "I'm going running. I've got a lot of heavy thinking to do, and I always do my best thinking when I'm running."

"You're going running? Now, when you should be working on the best thing that has ever happened to you? Are you out of your mind?" Flo stared at her.

"It's good for me," Deena answered.

"But it's hot out there," Flo said.

"I've got cool clothes and I can use the shower in the office," Deena said.

"I don't understand it. You run home every evening," Flo said, shaking her head. "That's a mile. Isn't that enough?"

Deena smiled. "Sometimes yes, sometimes no. Today it's not enough."

"But you should be thinking about skyscrapers."

"The stone giants?" Deena said. "I think about them all the time."

* * *

Ed James, another architect with Conway-Hill, was waiting at the elevator when Deena walked over to it. The heavy man with thick, yellow hair and blue eyes gave Deena an angry nod, stared at her running clothes for a second, and then turned away.

Deena could feel Ed's anger as she waited for the elevator without saying a word. It seemed to sit on the air like a dark cloud. The most important job to come Conway-Hill's way *ever*—and Deena LaSalle had it.

Deena thought that every architect in the company would probably be jealous. But she hadn't thought it would show up so soon. She knew the others would be upset that they hadn't been given the job. And it must be worse for Ed James. He would have to finish the work on the King Steak Restaurant plans. It couldn't be any fun taking over another person's designs.

Suddenly Ed turned to her. "You don't have it yet, you know."

"I think I do," Deena said in a calm voice. She was going to keep her cool no matter what.

He started to speak again, but then the elevator doors opened. Ed stood to one side to let Deena go in first. Then he changed his mind and walked in ahead of her. For a moment Deena thought of waiting for the next elevator. The doors started to close.

No, she thought, putting her hand out to stop the doors. I'm not going to let people push me around. I have as much right to design that building as anyone else does. She boarded the elevator. The doors closed as she turned to face them.

No one spoke for the next few moments. Then Ed piped up, "You really are the little favorite, aren't you?" He spoke in a voice that had a mean sound to it.

"Am I?" Deena asked. "I just thought I was a good architect."

Ed gave a short laugh. "There are lots of good architects here. But the little favorite got the State Bank. You and Conway must be very good friends."

"Being friends has nothing to do with anything," Deena said. "I've been working for Conway for seven years," she stated. "He knows what I can do."

"Seven years! You really think seven years is time enough to learn your job?"

The elevator came to a stop on the first floor. Deena wasn't going to waste any more time talking with Ed. She started to step out through the open doors. But he called to her.

"Is that the latest look?" he asked, staring at Deena's clothes.

"It is if you're going running." Deena gave Ed a sweet smile. "You might try running a bit yourself. With your feet, that is—instead of your mouth."

Without another word, Ed stepped out of the elevator and walked away.

Well, if that's a taste of what's going to happen to me, Deena thought, I'd better be ready for it. She pushed through the doors that led to the street. The hot July sun beat down on her. Not the best time to run, she thought to herself. But she needed the easy feeling that only running could bring to her mind and body. She needed to think about the excitement of the day and to let it all sink in.

I won't push it, she told herself, as she did some bends and stretches. I'll just take it nice and easy. She started running at a slow, lazy

pace, moving through the thinning lunch crowd.

No one stared at her as she ran. She wasn't the only New Yorker out for a run that day.

She ran and ran, enjoying the feeling of life that coursed through her. She moved lightly down the side streets and looked at the different faces that hurried by. Dark glasses and bright clothes. Laughing and quick talk.

The sun was playing tricks again. It was sending long fingers of light between the gray buildings.

Deena moved toward the light. But just as she was about to reach one of the fingers, it moved back and hid behind a stone giant—or a cloud. Then another finger of light jumped out just ahead of her. She moved down the street toward it, though she knew it would be gone by the time she got there. It was.

One day, she thought, as her feet tapped the hot ground—one day, I'm going to catch the sun.

Going in Circles 3

"Ideas," Deena said to herself that evening in her apartment. "I have a hundred ideas—but which one is the right one?"

She had only until October to work through her ideas and get the State Bank design and model ready. Four months was not a lot of time.

Deena was deep in thought when the telephone rang. Her friend Emily Peterson was calling.

"Did you get it?" Emily asked at once, in an excited voice.

"How did you know?" Deena said. She was surprised that her friend knew about the job already.

"It was in the mail when I got home," Emily said.

"Hold everything," Deena said. "Are we talking about the same thing?"

"The New York City Marathon," Emily almost shouted. "Did you get the papers yet? Did you sign up for the race?"

"Oh, that," Deena said. "Yes, I got all that stuff. It came in the mail today."

"Well? Aren't you even a little bit excited?"

"I'm returning it," Deena told her in a quiet voice. She put her feet up on her white desk. "I won't be using it."

"You're what?" Emily's voice rang out. "You've waited all year for that piece of paper. Now you're sending it back! Would you care to explain that to me?"

Deena let out a long breath. What she was about to say was hard for her. "I can't run in the marathon after all. It's not possible."

"You can't mean what you're saying." Emily sounded very angry. "What's standing in your way?"

Deena tried to explain. "Listen, Emily, the best thing has happened. I'm going to design the State Bank Building. It's going to take up all my time. But it's the building all of the architects have been talking about and trying to get their hands on. And your old friend, Deena LaSalle, got the job. Are you surprised?"

Emily waited a second before giving her answer. Then she spoke. "Why should I be surprised?" she asked. "You've worked hard, and you're good. But why should your job keep you out of the marathon? I don't think it's fair."

"It's a 60-story building, Emily," Deena said. "I'll need every minute I've got to work on it. Training for the marathon would take up too much time."

"But this won't be the first building you've ever designed," Emily said.

"True, but this one has to be ready in October. Since the marathon is being held the same month, I just don't think I'll have time for both."

"You should give yourself the chance," Emily said. "Besides, I need you to train with."

Emily, a high school physical education teacher, had run the marathon twice before. She had finished the long, hard course both times—all 26 miles and 385 yards of it. Her time, however, had been over four hours. The winner's time in the women's class was close to two and a half hours.

Emily's goal this year was to race the course in under three and a half hours. And she had planned to train and race with Deena. Deena, too, had run the marathon two times before. But she had not been able to finish either time. Deena had been training with a different goal. She wanted to run the marathon this time from start to finish. Speed was not important, but she had hoped to finish within four hours.

Thinking back to all the work they had already done, Deena didn't know what to say. She wanted to race. She wanted to reach her goal. But now that the marathon was getting closer, the training would take up more and more of her time. "Look," she said at last, "I'm not going to give up running. I'd never do that. It helps me wind down after work. It helps me think. It keeps me fit. I'll run with you as often as I can, Emily. But you'll just have to understand that the State Bank Building is a marathon in itself."

"All I know is that you'll be sorry if you give up this race," Emily told her. "You'll have to wait a whole year to try again."

Deena took a deep breath. She knew she could complete the marathon—if she could just keep up her training.

"Give me some time to think about it," she said. "I'll call you tomorrow."

"I'll only want one answer from you," Emily said in a strong voice.

"I know that," Deena told her. "But I can only do so much."

After she put the telephone down, Deena looked out the window. She knew the job was more important than the race. She had been asked to do something good for her city. What she did for State Bank was also for the people of New York. She had to please them—and herself—by coming up with a building that was nice to look at, to work in, and to visit. It was a tall building—and a tall order.

No, there's no way I can do all that and still train for the marathon, she thought. I'm being chicken. I should have told Emily no right away. There will be other marathons. The building has to come first.

She sat back in her chair. But I want to race, she thought. I want to race so much I can almost taste it. If only the building had not come along! Then she shook her head and smiled. "I must be mad to think of such a thing," she said to herself.

You have a race, she thought. It's a race to finish the building. Let it go at that. You can still run when there's time. You can run in the race even if you haven't trained enough. If you don't finish, no one will send you to jail.

She shook her head again. No, it's all or nothing. I can't run, and that's that.

She looked out her window again. The stone giants looked back at her.

CHAPTER 4

Make a Bet

She was running through the cool, green forest. The trees seemed to bend toward her, waving their long, dark arms. It was as if they wanted to grab her . . . to hold her there . . . to keep her in the woods forever. The sound of birds rang out clear as a bell. She closed her eyes against the sound.

Clear as a bell. The clock next to Deena's bed was ringing as if it would never stop. Deena reached out to shut it off. The dream was almost gone. For a second, she tried to catch it again. What was it? She was a little girl running through the forest. Was she running away from something? Toward something? She still didn't know.

Shaking her head, Deena climbed out of bed. Though it was a clear, bright morning, she had the feeling that something was wrong. It was something other than the dream. Her job? No, that wasn't it. And then it came to her. The marathon. Emily wanted an answer.

"OK," she said to herself, "I've made up my mind. The building comes first. It's what I've been waiting for. The marathon goes." She went to the telephone, but she stopped short of calling Emily.

Why start the day on a low note? she thought. I'll call her from work. My head will be clear by then. I'll tell her no, and that will be that.

* * *

Flo Adams was already at her desk when Deena came in. Deena made a face as her assistant bit into a big sweet roll.

"Good morning," Deena said. "Any calls yet?"

"A hundred of them," Flo said, handing her some slips of paper.

Holding the notes, Deena went into her office and sat down at her desk. The calls were from Conway, Ed James, and a few other people in the office. Emily had called too.

"Well, Emily's in school now. I won't be able to get her until this afternoon," she called through the open door to Flo.

"I know," Flo answered. "She was hoping to catch you before she had her first class. Something wrong?"

Deena shook her head. "Not really. She wants me to run in the marathon with her, that's all."

"The marathon! Fine. Just what you need."

"Don't worry. I'm not going to do it, so let's just forget about it," Deena said. "Come on, we've got work to do."

* * *

Deena stayed at her desk right through lunch. She had a lot of studying to do before she could begin drawing. She needed to know the city laws that set the rules for how wide the skyscraper could be. She had to plan the inside space, the building shell, and the stone that would cover it. There was a lot to learn and to think about.

She was deep in work when Flo came to her office door after lunch.

"Can I come in for a second?" Flo asked. She had a worried look on her face.

"Sure thing. Pull up a chair."

Flo held a soft drink in her hand. "Did you eat?" she asked.

"I had it sent up from downstairs," Deena said. Finally she looked up at Flo. Then she stared. "What's the matter?" she asked. "You look worried."

"I was in the hall," Flo said. "I heard something I thought maybe you should know."

Deena turned back to her work. "What's the problem?" she asked.

"You had better listen," Flo said.

Deena looked up again. She saw that Flo had something important to say—and that it wouldn't wait. She put her pencil down. "OK, out with it. What's the matter?"

"People are saying things."

"What things?" Deena asked. She thought she probably knew already.

"Things like you got the State Bank job because—because of your close ties with Conway, to put it in simple words."

Deena laughed. "Oh those are simple words all right. Ed James pulled the same thing with me yesterday. I didn't let it get to me then. And I won't let it get to me now.

People can think what they want. Gilbert is my friend. His wife is also a good friend of mine."

"I know that," Flo said. "I'm only telling you what I heard."

"I don't have to explain myself to anyone," Deena said in an angry voice.

"Hey, I'm on your side," Flo told her. "But that's not the whole story. The thing I'm afraid of is the bet."

"Bet?" Deena looked hard at Flo. "What bet?"

"The bet that everyone in the office is in on. The bet that you won't finish the building on time, and that Conway or someone else will have to take over. And that even if you finish, the bank people won't like it."

"That's a pretty silly bet, and no one should make it," Deena said. "Gilbert Conway always lets young architects take on hard jobs. He's known for that. That's why we all work here. He thinks that New York needs a new look, and that I can do that by designing the State Bank Building. And I'm going to. I'm going to come up with a great design, and no one is going to have to finish it for me."

Flo kept watching Deena. "You know it, and I know it. But no matter what you and Conway say, everyone else is still making bets. That's a fact, Deena."

Deena sat for a second, deep in thought. Then she spoke up. "They all wanted the job, and I got it. Now they're jealous, but that's their problem." She looked up at Flo. "I'm sure Ed James is behind the betting. He's angry, and he would like to see me fall flat on my face. Well, I'm not going to. Instead, I'm going to design the most beautiful building in New York. And I'm going to do something else. I'm going to run the marathon too. I'll show Ed James. And I'll show anyone else who wants to watch me. They'll see just how much I can do when I put my mind to it."

CHAPTER 5

Getting Set

It was past five o'clock when Flo walked into Deena's office later that day. The sky was still bright, but shadows were beginning to fall across Deena's desk.

"It's after five, Deena," Flo said. "If you're not going to go home, at least take a break. Tell me about the marathon."

Deena pushed her work to one side and smiled. "Good idea. I need a break." She pulled a map of the marathon course out of her desk and looked at it. Then she looked across at Flo. "Really want to know about it?"

Flo nodded. "Know about it, yes. Run it, no."

Deena laughed. "Well, to begin with, a marathon is a footrace over an open course.

The course is 26 miles and 385 yards long."

Flo seemed surprised. "That's a long way. But why the 385 yards?"

"It has to do with something that happened long ago. There was a war between the Greeks and the Persians. The Greeks won. A runner ran all the way from the city of Marathon to Athens to tell about it."

"And that distance was 26 miles and 385 yards," Flo said.

"Well, more or less. I think the miles we run now are different. But any time a marathon is run these days, the course is 26 miles and 385 yards long."

Flo thought for a minute. "You know, I think I've heard about that first run from Marathon before. And I remember something about it. When the runner got to Athens, he dropped dead. Very nice to know about the dropping dead part."

"He wasn't in shape," Deena said, grinning.

"You'll be in shape, I suppose."

"Look, Flo, that Greek runner wasn't taking part in a race. He had to get to Athens, and that was that. I don't have to get to Athens. I don't even have to finish the race. I can always drop out, give up. I'll just do what I can do."

"I know you," said Flo. "You won't give up. Not this time. Not now that you've made up your mind to finish. You'll do it. Even if you fall on your face. You're running against everyone in this office. Only they'll be standing still. You'll be knocking yourself out."

"The only person I'll be running against is Deena LaSalle. I know what 'm doing," Deena said in an even voice.

"I give up," Flo said, throwing her arms into the air. She turned to the map. "It starts at the Verrazano Bridge on Staten Island, right?"

"Right. And there'll be 14,000 racers."

"There may be 14,000 to start, but I'll bet there won't be many to finish."

"Flo, cut it out," Deena said. "I'm going to finish and so will a lot of other people. People run in marathons all over the country, and they finish all the time."

"OK, OK," Flo said. "Let's see now. It looks like the course goes through a part of each of the five boroughs of New York. Nice little sight-seeing trip."

"You don't see any sights, believe me," Deena told her. "All you see are your feet hitting the street and the blue line down the center of the road."

Flo looked harder at the map. "Here's a note that says 20 miles. Staten Island never seemed that far away from the Bronx."

"It's 20 miles all right. The course just winds around a lot." Deena laughed. "It will seem a lot longer when I'm running it. But any good runner should be able to make it to that 20-mile spot. *If* she or he is in good shape. But at that point, it gets really hard."

"I think I've heard about that," Flo said. "When you're so tired you can hardly move. Isn't it called 'hitting the wall'?"

Deena nodded again. "It takes a strong will to go on, when your body has had it. There can be a lot of pain. But if you've trained right, you know you can do it. Even if you want to stop and give up, sometimes you can't. Something keeps you going." She waited a second, remembering her last two marathon tries. Then she added, "I hope."

CHAPTER 6

By the Book

Deena and Emily Peterson had known each other since high school. They had first met on their school's track team. And they had stayed friends through their years at City University. But, after that, they had lost touch. Deena had gone to work for Conway-Hill. Emily had married and had moved away. After a few years, she left her husband and moved back to New York.

They had met again by chance at the New York Road Runners Club. They had kept up their running and decided to run together two or three times a week. Now they were training for the marathon together. Their plan went by the book. They were mixing days of hard running with days of easy running. They would run 3 miles one evening. The next evening they would run 9 miles. After that 18. Then back down again. Then they would slowly add to each of those distances. They knew that the body needs to rest at some points so that it can take on more and more.

The pace Deena ran with Emily was easy enough for talking. That was by the book too. Running did not mean losing one's breath. If you could talk as you ran, you were holding a good pace and not going too fast. With a strong but even pace, you could run a lot longer. That was what Deena wanted. But Emily was thinking about speed as well. At some point she would push on to better her time.

Right now they were running and talking—running down the long, dark streets of the city. The tall buildings, the giants of stone, seemed to bend toward them, watching. Watching and waiting.

Emily had a question as her red running shoes hit the street. "How do they feel about the marathon? At work, I mean."

Deena did not say anything for a moment. When she did speak, the words had nothing to do with Emily's question. "If this were the reservation, I'd like it better."

Emily was surprised for a second, but then shook her head slowly and smiled. She knew of her friend's feeling for the reservation. "We can always run in Central Park," Emily said. "It's a beautiful park. We don't have to run along the streets."

"No, this is OK," Deena said. "I'm used to it. Only sometimes I want to close my eyes. And then open them to find the buildings gone."

"I thought you liked New York," Emily said.

"I do and I don't," Deena said. "I dream of the reservation a lot, you know. My whole family is there, and I'm here."

"But you grew up on the streets of New York," Emily said. "This is your home. Not the reservation upstate."

"I can dream about it, though," Deena said. "On hot nights like tonight, I can dream about it. I haven't been there in a long time, you know. And I miss it."

Emily listened to the sounds their shoes made on the hot street. "Sometimes I think you run because you plan to keep on running one day, Deena LaSalle. All the way to the reservation."

Deena didn't speak for a minute. She seemed lost in thought. She finally said, "Maybe that's just what I plan to do."

"Not until you build your building, though, I think."

Deena laughed her thoughts away. "Oh, that stone giant! He's giving me trouble."

Now it was Emily's turn to laugh. "You're not kidding, are you? You think a stone giant is after you."

"It's an Onondaga legend," Deena told her. "One of my grandmothers told it to me when I was a kid."

"Did it frighten you?" Emily asked.

"Maybe. I'm not sure. Would you like to hear it?"

"No way to stop you, is there?" Emily asked.

"That's right. I've been dying to tell it to someone," Deena said, laughing again. "It goes like this. The Stone Giant was once like other men. He loved to eat, though—a little like my assistant, Flo Adams, in fact. I guess after a while he ate everything in sight, so he started to eat human beings. He began to grow. His skin turned hard, as hard as stone. The Onondagas found they couldn't kill him, no matter what they tried. Every day he ate another human being. My people decided they had to come up with a plan to kill him. They built a road to the marsh. There they dug a great hole. Then they covered it with branches from trees. The next day when the giant went looking for something to eat, an Onondaga led him down the road. The giant fell into the trap, and that was that."

"Great story," said Emily, looking over at Deena. "But he was killed. How can he still be after you?"

Deena smiled. "He came back. The Onondagas have plenty of stone giant stories."

"I don't want to hear them," Emily said. Then she cried out, and suddenly she was on the ground holding her foot. She hadn't seen an old can on the street and had fallen over it. Deena could see that she was in pain.

"I think I've broken something." Emily took a deep breath. "Oh, I can't believe this. I think I'm out of the race."

CHAPTER 7

Keeping Up the Pace

Gilbert Conway was pacing his office when Deena came in. "Sit down," he said when he saw her. He walked over to his desk and waited while she pulled up a chair.

"I hear you plan to run the marathon," he said as soon as she sat down. "I can't have you training and designing the State Bank Building at the same time. It's either one or the other, but not both."

Deena shook her head. "I can do both. I'll train for the race. And I'll have the plans to you in time for a model to be made and presented by the middle of October.

"No. You'll have to give up running for the time being," Conway said, hitting his desk hard. "What you think you can do and what you can do aren't the same thing."

Now Deena started to get angry too. "What I do with my own time is my own business, Gilbert," Deena said. "You can only talk to me about my work. I'm not falling down on the job, am I?"

Conway gave her a hard smile. "If you keep running, you may do just that."

"I know how to run," Deena told him. "I'm not going to hurt myself." Then she felt her face grow hot. Emily had hurt herself—her foot had a small break in it. Emily was out of this year's marathon, but she was going to coach Deena instead.

Conway kept looking at her. "I just want you to have the time to design the best building possible," he said.

Deena stood up. She kept her voice under control. "I will. And you'll get the plans on the day you need them. The best plans possible. Just stay cool. I know what I'm doing."

Conway sat down on the corner of his large desk and rubbed his eyes. "You'd better," he said. "A lot is riding on you, you know."

* * *

"It's raining, Emily. I'm not going running tonight. Besides, there is still a lot I have to do. Things are beginning to pile up for me."

"What?" Emily screamed into the telephone. "I won't hear of it. Do your warm-up stretches, and get out there. It's only 3 miles tonight. Is that too much to ask?"

"Yes," Deena said.

"You heard me. Get going." She hung up.

Deena took a deep breath as she put down the telephone. "I like to run," she said to herself. "Winter or summer, rain or shine. I do like to run. I really do."

* * *

"Say, sister, where are you going?" The voice came out of the growing dark. It was somewhere behind her.

Deena kept moving. She had heard that line before. It could mean trouble. She picked up speed and moved out into the center of the street. The lights of a car might send the caller away. And in the street she would be far away from the shadows and dark places between buildings.

The footsteps kept ringing behind her. "Where are you going in such a hurry?" the man called again.

Deena kept moving. Though the rain had stopped, the street was still wet. She hoped she wouldn't slip.

"Hey, come on," the voice called once more. This time the man sounded out of breath. "Wait for me!"

"I'm heading for the police station," Deena called over her shoulder. "Want to come along?"

The footsteps dropped off. Deena raced down the street. She would finish the 3 miles. And tomorrow the 9 miles. And after that, 18.

* * *

"Nine miles tonight." Emily's voice sounded bright on the telephone. "It's even nice outside. No rain. Plenty of sun."

"Sun?" Deena asked. "The sun's always gone when I get there. The stone giants hide it."

"Don't tell me about it. Do your warming up and get going."

"But it's 9 miles," Deena said. "By myself. I need someone to talk to."

"Talk to yourself."

"I'm not very funny," Deena said.

"Then run in Central Park," Emily told her. "You'll find plenty of funny people training there."

"No," Deena laughed. "I'll run here, the way I always do. I live here and work here. I'll run here too."

"That's right," Emily said. "Run where the stone giants can grab you."

Deena looked out her window and made a face. "That's not all that tries to grab me," she said.

* * *

"Tonight you run hills," Emily said. "You need to get ready for running over the Queensboro Bridge. It's like climbing a hill."

Deena made a tired sound. "But every part of my body hurts already."

"Then just stretch more," Emily said as she reached for another roll. It was Friday morning and she was having breakfast with Deena. "Do more warm-ups and cool-downs."

"I do a lot as it is."

"Do more," Emily said with a smile.

"Yes, Coach."

CHAPTER 8

A Circle of Light

Where had the time gone? Suddenly it was the middle of September. The marathon was only a month away. And so was the date when the plans and the model for the State Bank Building would be given to the head of State Bank.

Training was going well. The design had been finished. But there was still one problem. Deena was not very happy with her design.

It was what State Bank wanted, she knew that. And it would be a good-looking building. It was to be high and square, with lots of floor space. Deena planned for white stone and big windows of smoked glass to cut the sun. A ring of water would circle the bottom of the building. There would be places for people to sit. It would be a striking giant. But the problem was that it wasn't special. The special idea Deena had hunted for had never come.

Maybe I *have* been too busy running, Deena thought as she looked at the plans once more.

There was a quick knock at her office door. Deena looked up. Ed James walked in. He threw Deena's plans for the King Steak Restaurant on her desk.

"Thought you'd like them back," he said, pulling at his bright tie. "I didn't use them. I started over on my own."

Deena smiled at him. He was trying to get to her. "I'm really sorry you couldn't use them," she said in a calm voice. Didn't want to, she thought.

Ed stared at her. He was waiting for her to blow her top. Then he smiled back. "If you're in a jam with the State Bank Building, you know you can always call me."

Deena acted as if she hadn't heard him. She reached for the King Steak plans and put them away. "I'll hold on to these," she said. "You may find you need them after all."

Ed grinned. "I won't, believe me. King Steak is very happy with my work."

Deena nodded. "Good, I'm glad. Now, is there anything else I can do for you?"

"No, I just came by to see if you needed help. I hear you're so busy running, you're in trouble with the plans."

Deena kept her cool. "You shouldn't believe everything you hear. You know how people talk. I even heard something about a bet."

Ed began to back out of her office. He suddenly acted as if the room had become too warm. "Well, see you," he said. "Call me if you need help."

Deena gave him a wide grin. "I'll do that, Ed. I really will."

* * *

Deena was running slow and easy. It was early Saturday morning. The day was clear but not hot yet. It was the time of week Deena liked best. The streets were almost empty of cars and people, and the big buildings and small stores sat quietly. Deena felt as if she owned the streets and the city itself.

Her feet pounded on, an even beat on the just-cleaned street. Her breath came in an easy rhythm. She felt strong, full of power and life. The half hour she had been running seemed like only a few minutes.

Though she was sweating and working hard, she felt cool and at peace. She might have been running in a forest, like the little girl in the dream. Deena smiled as she saw how easy it was to bring a forest right in among the stone giants of the big city. You just ran, and there you were in a forest.

And then it came to Deena.

"Of course," she said to herself. Her smile grew bigger, but she did not stop running. It was the special idea that had been missing. It must have been there all along, only hiding. It was the special idea that she needed for her stone giant, the State Bank Building.

It was all so simple. A stone giant—and at its feet, a cool, green forest. Deena had to laugh. It was her reservation, and it had been waiting for her. It had just taken clearing her head to find it.

She thought on. The water would still circle the outside of the building. Inside, though, behind great walls of glass, would be the forest. It would fill the whole street floor, from

Greenwich to Beach. It would be State Bank's present to the people of New York. A green forest to be enjoyed all year long.

Deena could see it already. Above the forest, the building would sit like a great mountain. The sun's fingers could find their way down that mountain. The fingers could touch the forest and the earth below.

"They'll like it," Deena whispered to herself. "I know that." She found herself slowing down to a walk and then to a stop. She stood for a minute, breathing hard and thinking about what had happened. It was as if she had run through a door. Beyond that door was a world where everything was right. She looked around. The street was the same, only a few people walking their dogs. But something was different. Deena looked down. She had come to a stop in a circle of light.

CHAPTER **9**

The Marathon

Time: 10:30 A.M.

Place: Verrazano-Narrows Bridge, Staten
Island

Crowds of people had come to watch the
marathon. There would be more people lining
the course. They would have ice and water
and drinks for the runners. There were funny
T-shirts and lots of laughs. The race was like
a giant picnic, with all of New York joining in.

Excitement was high near the starting line.
The air was thick with it. The big day touched
everyone—those who came to watch, and
those who came to run.

Then, when it seemed not another runner
could jam into the crowd, the gun went off.
A great shout went up from the people.

The New York City Marathon had begun.

Almost 14,000 racers—Deena LaSalle among them—headed through the starting line.

But she almost hadn't started. When she had been doing her warm-ups with Emily, she had been worried. "I'm beginning to have second thoughts about running," she had said.

Emily's mouth had dropped open. "Are you kidding?"

"No, I'm beginning to wonder what I'm doing here," Deena said. "I keep thinking about my building plans and wondering if the State Bank people will like them."

Emily shook her head. "Don't think about that now. You have a race to run. I only wish I were running in your place." Her foot was better now, but she was in no shape to run a marathon. Emily was a little sad, but she had worked to get Deena excited about the race.

It had helped. When it was time to line up, Deena was feeling good about running.

"Go at your own pace," Emily had shouted to her. "I'll wait for you at the Queensboro Bridge." The rest of her words had been lost in the noise as the runners had started forward.

* * *

Time: 12:00 noon

Place: Bedford Avenue, Brooklyn

Ten miles down—16 miles and 385 yards to go. Deena was in good shape. She was running at an even pace, and she didn't feel any pain yet. She was worried, though, that her time might be a little slow. She wanted to finish the marathon in under four hours.

* * *

At the 11-mile point, Deena got her running time. She had been right. Her time was a little slow. She had been running nine-minute miles. If she wanted to finish the race safely under four hours, she would have to bring up her speed.

"Want some?"

Deena looked to the right. A boy wearing a hat that said "I Love New York" was holding out a piece of ice to her. She nodded, and took the ice in her hand.

"Good luck," the boy called after her.

"Thanks," she waved back.

She put the ice in her mouth and kept on running. She pushed a little harder. As she moved, she could see that the crowd of runners had begun to thin out. Some had moved on ahead. Some were slowing down. Some would soon begin to drop out.

* * *

Time: 12:40 P.M.
Place: Queensboro Bridge, Queens

Now it was 15 miles down and 11 miles 385 yards to go. Deena reached the foot of the bridge and moved to the side to stop. She had started to hurt and was breathing hard. Her legs felt thick and heavy. She also had a sore spot on her right heel.

She tried to catch her breath as she looked around for Emily. Her red-headed friend was making her way through the crowd with a drink of water.

"You're doing great," she smiled.

Deena tried to smile back. "Sure," she said. But it wasn't true. She looked up at the bridge. It seemed as high and as hard to climb as Mount Everest. Even with the red and blue rug that had been put down to cover the iron tracks of the bridge, getting across it would be a real test of what she could do.

"Your time is pretty good," said Emily as Deena finished the drink. "Don't push any harder. You'll come in under four hours at the pace you're going."

"That's good to know," Deena said. "That's if I keep going. I've got a sore spot on my heel. I've got to take off my shoe."

"OK, take it easy. We'll cover up the sore spot so your shoe won't rub it."

Deena found a place to sit down and started pulling off her shoe. Runners crowded in around her. They were all stopping before making the mile-long climb over the bridge.

With the shoe off, Deena checked her sore heel. It looked bad. But Emily just covered it up as if it were nothing. "Listen," she said. "You can still do it. Walk over the bridge if you have to. Remember, the idea is to finish the race. It might be smart just to forget the four-hour mark."

"The way I feel now, I could forget about running completely," said Deena. She wiped off the sweat that was running down her neck.

"You don't mean that," Emily said. "Look, don't think about time. Just think about getting to the finish line."

"OK," Deena said. "I will. And I'll get there." She stood up and took a deep breath. "And I'll cross that bridge running."

* * *

It was hard. Deena's legs hurt, and her heel was still sore. But she kept at it. Slowly, very slowly, she ran toward the top of the bridge.

But it seemed so far away. If only she could make it over the top to the downhill side. She looked out across the water for a second. The great buildings of Manhattan stood waiting there for her to reach them. The stone giants looked like an army—and they seemed to be staring at her.

Deena looked back. "No, I won't give up," she told them.

The Stone Wall *10*

Time: 1:20 P.M.
Place: 135th Street, the Bronx

It was the 20-mile point. There were only 6 miles and 385 yards to go. But Deena LaSalle had hit the stone wall. Her body felt as if it belonged to someone else.

She came to a dead stop at the mark. It did not seem possible that she could go on. She was breathing hard. Sweat was streaming down her face and neck. Her legs were like lead. She would have to tell Emily that it was all over.

In a minute, Emily came up to her with a drink in her hand. She helped Deena over to the side and gave her a wet rag. Deena wiped herself down and then put the rag on her head.

"Emily," she said. "It's too much."

"Calm down and sit here," Emily told her. "You're going to finish. Your time is good, did you know that?"

"I don't care," Deena said. She dropped down on the hot sidewalk and closed her eyes. It would be so nice to pack it all in. She just did not think she could take one more step. "My heel is too sore," she said. She was like an engine that had run down. There was no way to start it again.

Emily helped her take her shoe off. "Don't worry about this. We'll get it fixed up," she said. Then, to take Deena's mind off the sore spot, she added, "Guess who came over to see how you were doing?"

Deena didn't answer. It didn't matter. She sat looking down at the ground.

"Come on," said Emily in a bright voice. "Take a guess."

"Whoever they are, ask them if they drove," Deena said slowly. "Maybe they can take me home."

"I'll tell you, if you won't guess. Flo Adams, Gilbert Conway, and—now you've got to guess."

Deena looked at Emily. "OK, who?"

"Ed James." Emily seemed pleased with herself.

Deena made a face. "You'll pull anything to get me to finish."

"Come on. Ed said something about losing the bet."

Deena stared at Emily. Then she took a deep breath. "That means State Bank liked my plans." She wanted to get excited, but she couldn't. She hurt too much all over. "I'm afraid to press down on my heel" was all she said.

"Stop thinking about it, Deena. Look, there were two things you wanted to do. You wanted to design a great building. And you wanted to finish the marathon. It looks like you've reached the State Bank goal, but how about the marathon? Do you really think you should give up now?"

Deena took another deep breath and rubbed her leg. "All right. All right. Give me a few more minutes. I'll try again."

* * *

Deena stepped on her heel. Pain shot up her leg. She took another step. Even that hurt. There's no way I can do it, she thought. No way.

But she moved out into the street. Something made her go. The blue line was there, and she had to follow it.

She tried different ways to run. She found that if she didn't press down too hard on the bad heel—if she let her foot fall a little to the inside—it hurt less. Less, but it still hurt.

She kept going. Soon a runner passed her. It was someone she knew.

"Keep up the good work," he called. Deena couldn't answer. But she could see he was in trouble too.

She went on, looking for the point when she would move past pain into peace. Everyone said that that time always came. But she was not there yet.

* * *

Time: 1:47 P.M.

Place: Central Park, Manhattan

It was the 23-mile point. There were 3 miles and 385 yards to go.

Deena was running in a cool, green forest. The sun was shining through the trees. She could almost touch it. But then she saw the stone giants watching her. Her dream and the marathon race through Central Park were mixing together.

Someone handed her a cold drink. She hardly knew it as she poured the stuff into her mouth and threw the last bit over her head. All she knew was that she was still moving.

Crowds lining the road shouted to her. She almost didn't hear them. A small girl held up a sign with some writing on it. She had to look hard to read it. It told her there were 24 miles down, 2 miles and 385 yards to go.

It almost didn't sink in. Nothing did. Not the pain in her foot. Not the stiff, terrible tired feeling in her legs. She didn't know how she could still breathe in and out. She knew only that she was still running. In a way, she did not know if it was possible to stop.

* * *

Someone was calling to her. "Stop!" Deena heard the word, but she kept on running.

"Stop!" It came again. She turned. Emily was running next to her. "Deena, stop! Stop! It's over."

I can't, Deena thought. "I'm running the marathon," she tried to say, but the words wouldn't come. She kept moving forward.

"Deena, you've passed the finish line. You did it," Emily shouted. "You ran the marathon in under four hours."

Even then, Deena ran a few more steps before it all sank in. Then she knew. Slowly, she went down, hitting the ground in a soft fall.

Never again, she thought. Never again.

She wasn't down for long. Hands grabbed her and helped her to her feet.

"You'll have to move again sometime." Emily laughed and hugged Deena.

Deena hugged her back. Then she looked up to see Gilbert Conway and Flo Adams standing beside her.

"What can we do for you?" Flo asked quickly.

"All I want is a nice, cold shower," Deena told her.

Flo smiled. "And then a party. We have a lot to party about."

Ed James nodded. "And I'll be paying for it."

Deena smiled. Then she made a face as she pressed down on her heel. Everything still hurt, but now it didn't matter.

She turned to Emily. "About the marathon next year," Deena said. "We'll train for it together. If we work really hard, we can both finish in under three and a half hours." Deena took a deep breath. Then she looked up, past the buildings, at the sun. "Caught you," she said.